Social Media Marketing
Coffee Shop

Coffee Shop Marketing
Content to Post on
Facebook, Instagram, Twitter,
Websites & More

Danielle McCorkle

Copyright © 2020 Danielle McCorkle
All rights reserved.
ISBN: 9798617368989

COPYRIGHT

Copyright ©2020 by Danielle McCorkle. All rights reserved. No part of this publication may be reproduced, stored in a retrieval system or transmitted in any form or by any means, electronic, mechanical, photocopying, recording, scanning, or otherwise, except as permitted under Sections 107 and 108 of the 1976 United States Copyright Act, without the prior written permission of the Publisher. No patent liability is assumed with respect to the use of information contained herein.

Trademarks: Social Media Marketing Coffee Shop is a trademark of the author and may not be used without written permission. All other trademarks are the property of their respective owners. The author is not associated with any product or vendor mentioned in this book. The publisher and author cannot attest to the accuracy of this information. Use of terms in this book should not be regarded as affecting the validity of any trademark or service mark.

While the author has used their best efforts to prepare this book, they make no warranties or representations with respect to the accuracy or completeness of contents in this book and specifically disclaim any implied warranties of merchantability or fitness for a particular purpose. No warranty may be created or extended by sales representatives or written sales materials. The advice and strategies contained herein may not be suitable for your situation. You should consult with a professional where appropriate. The publisher and author shall not be liable for any loss of profit or any other commercial damages, including but not limited to special, incidental, consequential, or other damages. The fact that an organization or website is referred to in this work as a citation and/or a potential source of further information does not mean that the publisher and the author endorse the information the organization or website may provide or recommendations it may make. Further readers should be aware that internet websites listed in this work may have changed or disappeared between when this work was written and when it is read.

Every effort has been made to make this book as complete and as accurate as possible, but no warranty or fitness is implied. The information provided is on an "as is" basis. The author and publisher shall have neither liability nor responsibility to any person or entity with respect to any loss or damages arising from the information contained in this book or from the use of any programs accompanying it. Information and ideas have been obtained by the author. The author does not guarantee the accuracy, adequacy, or completeness of any information and is not responsible for any errors or omissions or the results obtained from the use of such information. All trademarks and copyrights mentioned herein are the possession of their respective owners and the author makes no claim of ownership by the mention of products that contain these marks.

CONTENTS

    Book Research   i

1. Social Media — Pg 1
2. Social Media Statistics — Pg 9
3. Social Media Calendar — Pg 11
4. Reaching Customers — Pg 19
5. Creative Posts — Pg 23
6. Beginning Phrases — Pg 26
7. Your Products — Pg 40
8. Coffee Content — Pg 55
9. Conversations — Pg 59
10. Events — Pg 63
11. Images — Pg 77
12. Your Business — Pg 89
13. More Content Ideas — Pg 97
14. # Hashtags — Pg 100
15. Resource Websites — Pg 112

    About the Author

BOOK RESEARCH

This book is based on the research of Facebook. Twitter, Instagram, and company websites for coffee shops and other businesses throughout the United States.

Thank you to all the hard-working people in the coffee industry who work tirelessly every day to make our lives better.

Thank you for purchasing this book. I hope it helps to grow your business exponentially!!

1 SOCIAL MEDIA

Chances are you are a super busy person concentrating on your business and working on growing your business. Whether you post once a week, daily, or more than once daily, you need great content to keep visitors coming back to your social media network or networks. Sometimes you may run out of good ideas, not have the time to commit to posting, or not think of the ideas listed in this book. I hope this book helps you grow your business exponentially and helps your customers. Please keep in mind, these are ideas and you alone must decide what is best for your business and your social media strategy.

WHY SOCIAL MEDIA?

Why is Social Media Important to your Business?

#1 Reason: It shows everyone including potential customers that you are still in business.

Additional Important Reasons

Great content brings people back to your sites for more visits and it gives you more opportunities to increase your sales.

It adds validity to your business that you are an expert in your field.

It is a quick way to promote your business. In turn, it is also a quick way to turn away customers without a good social media presence and poor content.

It is a time-taking endeavor but it is a free and vital part of the business you want to grow.

Customers who view your social media decide if they want to spend their money with you.

It is a great free referral service. Your social media may be used by folks who are researching companies for their own use as well as to share with friends, family members, and colleagues.

The content you post should be in your words and they follow your social media goals.

Social media is the way many folks get informed locally or if they are visiting the area in the future.

Social media gives you a chance to show your personality.

Your Social Media Goal(s)?

What is your social media goal

How are you going to accomplish this goal / these goals

How will each of your social media networks show your personality

Does your social media parallel your website

Set your goals with ways to use social media to boost your sales

How Often Should You Post?

How often to post depends on your business and your goals. Some businesses post daily. Some businesses post 1 time a week. Some businesses post every other week. Some businesses post as often as their competition. This is a decision that you need to make based on your business goals.

What Should You Post About?

What is most important about your business and social media is that social media's purpose is to generate sales for your business. Based on your business, experts recommend that you post a percentage of the time selling your products and the other percentage posting about non-selling content. However, you need to decide what is best for your business. If you are a restaurant, maybe you post 90 percent about your food with images. Maybe the other percentage is your business hours, your menu, when you are closed for any upcoming holidays. If you are a hair salon, maybe a larger percentage of your posts are about when you have open appointment times. If you are a real estate company, your posts may vary based on your listings. You may have a higher percentage of listing posts at different times throughout the year and the other times your posts are about your business, your community, your personality to reach more potential clients. Thus, it is your call regarding how often you post and about what. One way to bring in customers and show that you are an expert in your field, is by posting frequently asked questions about valuable content that your customers and potential customers usually ask.

Where does your content come from? You can either create your own content or include links to great content. Be sure to follow the legal rules for copyright, trademark, and other laws. It is very important to know the law regarding what you can and cannot as well as how to legally post.

Posting Content About Your Business

Let your posts show your business's personality

Post fun things about your business or your community

Post quotes or motivational messages

Post fun content that makes you chuckle

Drive your own narrative in your posts

Post what you are passionate about

There Are Different Ways To Post

Do you have a lot of words and information in the post or is it one to two sentences?

Do include your phone number, address, and company URL?

Do you add emojis?

Do you add other URLs?

Do you add hashtags?

Do you add other links to your other social media networks?

Are you incorporating other new ways to post on social media that is not available at the time this book was published?

Most important is the content that you are posting and the image(s) you use. Everything else is used to continue to generate sales and customers as well as potential customers visiting or sharing with others. Hopefully your content generates repeat visits, shares, and telling others to look at your social media posts.

The Importance Of Images

Social media networks are very visual. It is important to have good images to draw in customers or potential clients to your business. Clear images are super important. Make sure you use the current optimal size for posting images. With the correct image sizes, you will be able to create engaging images that sends a message about your brand, services, products, and business goals. Since the shape and dimensions with social media networks changes, you need to research the current upload sizes.

There are many graphic design companies that have online graphic-design tools for free or for a charge. These are awesome drag and drop formats that are formatted for the social media network you want to create an image for. Perfect for non-designers and busy business people.

SOCIAL MEDIA'S PURPOSE

The purpose of social media is to grow your business not put it out of business.

MAYBE DON'T POST ...

- Don't repeat posting the same website's articles even if they are very good, mix it up
- Don't repeat post the same images close together in time, it looks like your website is not current and you are recycling images because you don't have any new ones
- Don't post bad pictures
- Don't post anything that will alienate your customers
- Don't post anything that violates copyright laws
- Don't post derogatory messages
- Don't post swear or cuss words
- Don't post bad language
- Don't post misspellings and other typos, this is an English teacher's nightmare!
- Don't post about your personal views for example politics. You run the risk of a large percentage of customers taking their money and spending it at a different business, most likely one of your competitors

BUSINESS VS PERSONAL

Your Business Social Media Networks vs Your Personal Social Media Networks

If you are the face of the company, be sure your personal social media is completely appropriate for your business. Once customers meet you, they might go search out your personal social media accounts.

2 SOCIAL MEDIA STATISTICS

FACEBOOK SOCIAL MEDIA STATISTICS

- 71% of American adults use Facebook, source https://blog.hootsuite.com/facebook-statistics/
- 74% of high income earners use Facebook, source https://blog.hootsuite.com/facebook-statistics/
- 74% of Facebook users log in daily, source https://blog.hootsuite.com/facebook-statistics/
- 90 million small businesses use Facebook, source https://blog.hootsuite.com/facebook-statistics/

INSTAGRAM SOCIAL MEDIA STATISTICS

- 37% of American adults use Instagram, source https://blog.hootsuite.com/instagram-statistics/
- 11% of U.S. social media users shop on Instagam, source https://blog.hootsuite.com/instagram-statistics/
- 75.3% of U.S. businesses will use Instagram in 2020, source https://blog.hootsuite.com/instagram-statistics/

TWITTER SOCIAL MEDIA STATISTICS

- 22% of adults in the U.S. use Twitter, source https://blog.hootsuite.com/twitter-statistics/
- Tweets with hashtags gets 100% more engagement, source https://blog.hootsuite.com/twitter-statistics/
- 30 million of Twitter's daily users are American, source https://blog.hootsuite.com/twitter-statistics/

3 SOCIAL MEDIA CALENDAR

THE IMPORTANCE OF A SOCIAL MEDIA CALENDAR

The purpose of keeping a social media calendar is ...

You know when and what you are posting.

You can prepare ahead of time for special dates or sales for your business.

You can analyze your sales and review your marketing for any social media content you posted that might be successful.

You can review historical data to decide going forward how you want to proceed.

You can review when you posted last year and if you want to change timing, content and networks you used.

You can coordinate social media with other marketing goals and campaigns. By having a social media calendar, you can see ahead of time what is coming up for your business marketing plans. A social media calendar gives you time to think about and decide what you want to do.

Holidays and Days of Interest

Holidays
National days
Special dates to post about
Seasonality of your business
Birthdays and anniversaries of your business and team members

Plan out your marketing campaigns

Coordinate your social media with your website and other forms of marketing you use

There are many free and for a charge social media calendars available online. Find the one that works best for you and your business.

Social Media Marketing Coffee Shop

https://nationaldaycalendar.com/calendar-at-a-glance/
https://icalendars.net/celebrations/

Social Media Calendar - Content
Week of XX-XX-XXXX
Holidays, My Sales, National Days, Local Events
THIS WEEK: List themes you are posting about

Date	Monday	Tuesday	Wednesday
Facebook			
Instagram			
Twitter			
LinkedIn			
Pinterest			
YouTube			
Other			

Social Media Calendar
Week of XX-XX-XXXX
Holidays, My Sales, National Days, Local Events
THIS WEEK: List themes you are posting about

Date	Thurs	Fri	Sat	Sun
Facebook				
Instagram				
Twitter				
LinkedIn				
Pinterest				
YouTube				
Other				

Social Media Calendar - Images Used
Week of XX-XX-XXXX

Date	Monday	Tuesday	Wednesday
Facebook			
Instagram			
Twitter			
LinkedIn			
Pinterest			
YouTube			
Other			

Social Media Calendar – Images Used

Date	Thurs	Fri	Sat	Sun
Facebook				
Instagram				
Twitter				
LinkedIn				
Pinterest				
YouTube				
Other				

OR

Social Media Calendar – Images Used

Image	Date	Date	Date
Inside Photo			
Menu			
Staff			
To Go Cup			
By the Fireplace			

If you want to post certain hashtags frequently, set up a table to track when they were last used.

Example:
Business Name: Beans Coffee Shop
Location: Fargo, ND
Your specialties:

Hashtag	Date	Date	Date
#Beans			
#Beanscoffee			
#fargocoffee			
#coldbrew			
#latte			
#beansbrunch			

Create your own social media calendar or locate one that works best for you to plan your marketing strategy for the year.

HOLIDAYS and NATIONAL DAYS

January 1   New Year's Day
January 5   National Keto Day
January 11   National Milk Day
January 20   National Martin Luther King Jr Day
January 25   National Irish Coffee Day
January 31   National Hot Chocolate Day
February 14   Valentines Day
February 29   Leap Day

March Madness
March 2   National Read Across America Day, Dr Seuss's Birthday

March #   Daylights Savings Day, Second Sunday in March

March 14   National Pi Day
March 17   St Patrick's Day
March 20   First Day of Spring
April 1   April Fool's Day
April 7   National Coffee Cake Day
April National Library Week, 2nd Week of April
May   Kentucky Derby, First Saturday in May
May   Small Business Week, First Week in May
May   Teacher Appreciation Day, Tuesday of First Full Week of May

May   Teacher Appreciation Week, First Monday through Friday in May

May   Mother's Day, Second Sunday in May
May   Memorial Day, Last Monday in May
June 8   National Best Friends Day
June 20   Summer Begins
June   Father's Day, Third Sunday in June
July 4   Independence Day, 4th of July!
July 11   National Blueberry Muffin Day
August   National Friendship Day, First Sunday in August

August 4   National Chocolate Chip Cookie Day
August 9   National Book Lovers Day
August 21   National Senior Citizens Day

September 6   National Coffee Ice Cream Day
September 6   National Read A Book Day
September   Labor Day, First Monday in September
September 23   First Day of Fall, change annually
September 27   National Chocolate Milk Day
September 29   National COFFEE Day
October 7   National Frappe Day
October   National Coffee with a Cop Day, First Wednesday in October

October 14   National Dessert Day
October 28   National Chocolate Day
October 31   Halloween
November 1   National Author's Day
November 1   National Cinnamon Day
November   Daylight Saving Time Ends, First Sunday in November

November 3   National Sandwich Day
November 5   National Doughnut Day
November 11   Veterans Day
November 23   National Espresso Day
November 26   National Cake Day
November   Thanksgiving Day, Fourth Thursday in November

November   Black Friday, Day After Thanksgiving
November   Small Business Saturday, Day After Black Friday

November   National Game & Puzzle Week, Week of Thanksgiving

December 4   National Cookie Day

December 13   National Cocoa Day
December 15   National Cupcake Day
December 21   National Crossword Puzzle Day
December 20   First Day of Winter, Winter Solstice
December 23   Chanukah Begins, changes annually
December 24   Christmas Eve
December 25   Christmas Day
December 31   New Year's Eve

Each State has its own National Day. Find your state's national day by searching X state national day.

4 REACHING CUSTOMERS

WHAT SETS YOU APART IN YOUR LOCAL COFFEE MARKET?

If you have any of the below items, make sure you post about it often so that anyone can access your information if they are viewing your social media networks. Also, chances are that they will share or tell others about your available information. Include the URL that links this content to the available information in your social media posts.

App
Do you use an App where customers can order ahead and pickup? Do you use an App where customers can request a delivery? Do you use an App where customers can reserve space at your location, maybe a meeting room? Do you have an App that displays events happening at your location?

Downloads
Information you offer that is free or is available for a price

Blog
Write a blog with content that customers or potential customers would benefit from and then link the blog in your post which shows you have credibility in the coffee shop market

Creative Content
Create creative content using an online graphics arts tool. Purposes could be if you are closed due to weather or holidays. If you have upcoming new products, new events, or other great offerings that followers may want to watch for.

Bazaar and Small Businesses
Do you have local businesses come by for a bazaar where your customers can purchase their products?

eBooks
Create eBooks and have available on your website and link the URLs in your social media posts

Frequent Visitor Program
Explain how your Frequent Visitor Program works.

Newsletter
Your monthly newsletter

Online Store
Post if you have an online store selling your products.

Podcast Channel
Your podcast
Your company podcast
Any recommended podcasts

Seminars and Speakers
Post when you will be offering Seminars.
Topics could be how to make coffee, tastings, new flavors available, how to make products.
In addition, inviting speakers to come in and discuss topics that could benefit your customers such as local businesses, health topics, senior subjects, technology, travel, and more.

YouTube Channel
A company YouTube Channel.

Videos
Post your own videos
Facebook Live for informational purposes
Video of your menu or location
Funny humorous videos about various subjects

Additional Information
Other free materials

MARKETING

Plan your marketing strategy ahead of time. What will you post about, what channels will you use, and coordinate it with your website. In addition, coordinate it with your products, holidays, and sales you are running.

There are many email lists to get on in order to find out what is happening in your area. Also, you can pre-plan and schedule your emails ahead of time in order to make it super easy to have your marketing calendar all planned out well in advance. Write down what your multichannel marketing technique is and how you plan to implement it.

Possible Email Lists To Sign Up For

Email lists for things in your area such as national parks, free events, public places

Email lists for chamber of commerce events for example local sporting events, local business's events

Other Ideas

Find websites that have great content, locally, in your industry, and per subject matter.

5 CREATIVE POSTS

SOME POST EXAMPLES

Schedule regular posts and events to draw repeat customers in as well as first time customers

♡ JOIN US for ...
♡ 10:00-2:00 pm: Come by to taste for ...
♡ All Day: Your product on sale, discounts given for purchases that day 💲‼

😎 Live Show Friday ☕🍷
Please Join Us!
555 Coffee Way, Hometown
@ (your hashtag)

😊 New Flavor Reveal
It's a Hit! 🔥
Stop by 🍪

🤍🖤🖤🖤☕ DON'T MISS 🎤

🤍🤍🖤🖤☕ ART SHOW 🗨️

📞 Call us at 555-555-1212 for To Go Orders

☕🤍☕ NEW HOURS ☕🤍☕

😍 Latte Art 😎☕

👕👚 New Items Are In ❗

🖤 Try our tea drinks 🍓🫐🍒

☕ We deliver 🚗

☀️ Happy Sunny Day ☕
Today's Flavor Salted Caramel Frappe
-
-
-
#coffeelover #recharge #coffeeallday #muffins

Post Your Contact Information Based On Your Desired Frequency
Call/text/email us for more information –
(Your email address)
(your phone number)

🎁 Gift Card! 💝

>>>>> White Chocolate Raspberry <<<<<

🚗 TRY OUR DRIVE-THROUGH 🏁

💻 ORDER ONLINE 📱

🆓 🚚 Free Parking ‼

‼Valet Parking ❗🚗

🚚 We deliver‼ ☕ 🍲 🥐 🍰

6 BEGINNING PHRASES

If you are looking for a beginning to your post, here are some phrases.

Phrases

A favorite

Afternoon boost

Afternoon pick me up

A great weekend to

A latte a day

All day

Another

Are you ready to

Attention Coffee Lovers

Back by popular demand

Back to the grind

Beat the heat

Brunch vibes

Café vibes

Caffeine cravings

Caffeine + Protein

Check out our

Check out our story

Cheers to the

Coffee Exclusive!

Coffee O'Clock

Coffee time is the best time to

Cold brew vibes

Come by

Come join the fun!

Come warm up

Crucial Tips

Daily drink

Did you know

Did someone say

Discount on

Do's and Dont's

Don't miss

Double punch day!

Enjoy the final days of Summer

Enjoy the beginning of Spring

Enjoy the rest of

Espresso vibes

Expert

Fall Favorites

Fall in love

Find us on Uber Eats and GrubHub

Flavor of the day is

Fuel up

Get a free

Get frosty

Get in the Holiday Spirit

Get it while its hot

Good morning

Grab and go

Grab one of our specialty drinks and head to XXX

Happiness is

Happy coffee day

Happy X coffee lovers!

Happy finals week!

Happy first day of

Happy Holidays

Happy Holidays from your family at @your business link

Happy chilly day

Happy sunny day

Have a great day!

Have an amazing day

Having a blast

Herbal tea alert

Holiday week

Holiday weekend

How to maximize your

Important Tips

Indulge in

It's a hit

It's never too cold for

It's never too hot for

It's refreshing

It's simply delicious

Join us

Join us for a break from the rain, heat, snow

Just in time for …

Just right

Just the way you like it …

Kid tested

Kid approved

Latte vibes

Limited time

Live Show

Lunch Plans

Meetings are better with

Meet our

X Month is here!

Morning fuel

X Morning Joy

Morning motivation

Mornings are not so bad when …

Myths

Need a breakfast idea

Need a last minute gift

New drink alert

New donut alert

New items are in

New kid friendly drink alert

New muffin alert

New pastry alert

New Years Resolutions

Nothing says XXX like XXX

Not in the mood for

Official season for ...

On sale

XXX one day at a time

One cup at a time

One of our favorites

Order ahead

Order online

Our passion is

Pair it with

Patio season

Pencil us in

Perfection!

Pick me up ...

Please join us

Quote of the day

Ready for

Recharge

Refreshing drink

Rise & shine!

Say no more

Seasonal Hours

X Served with a smile

Share the love

Stop in and enjoy our AC

Stop in before they are gone

So much flavor

So much love

Start your busy week with us for a quick cup or to go

Start your morning right ...

Start your morning with

Stay tuned

Stop by to recharge …

Stop in for a

Stop in to say Hello and grab a cup!

Stop in to chill off (warm weather)

Stop in to take the chill off (cold weather)

Survived the heat wave

Take time for yourself Xday, Take time for yourself

The gangs all here

The perfect combination

The perfect shot

This is our

Thursday

Timeless

Time to recharge

'Tis the Season

Today's flavor is

Today only

Today we have

Tomorrow only

Treat yourself to

Try them all

Try our Featured Drink ...

Unique gifts

Warm drink vibes

We appreciate ...

We are up early for you

We are ready for

Welcome ...

We deliver

We love this community!!

We love you (your city)!

We spilled the beans ...

When in doubt

While it lasts

Work week mood

You asked for it

You deserve it

Yummy

Days Of The Week

Happy Monday

Monday Blues

Monday motivation

Come make your Monday better with a delicious drink

Cure for Mondays

Great Monday

Happy Monday

Mocha Monday

Rainy days and Mondays always makes me love coffee

Tuesday Tip(s)

Start your Tuesday with ...

Take on Tuesday

Happy Wednesday...

Hump day motivation

Wake up Wednesday

Happy Thursday

Throwback Thursday

Fridays

Frida-yeah

Friday Friendships

Friday Fuel

Friday Tasting

Friday vibes

Friday afternoon coffee break

Happy Friday

Happy Friday Everyone!

TGIF

Get ready for the weekend

Friends and coffee Saturdays

Happy Saturday

Happy Saturday Everyone

Lazy Saturday

Saturday afternoons

Saturday morning

Saturday morning coffee

Saturday stroll

Selfie Saturday

Simple Saturday

Super Saturday

Sweet Saturday

Good Morning Sunday

Sunday Best

Sunday Funday

Sunday morning

Selfie Sunday

Weekend!

Weekend breakfast

Weekend fuel

Weekend vibes

Weekends are better with

Ready for the weekend?

The weekend is here

This weekend

Welcome to the Weekend

Happy January

Welcome February

Hello March

April showers

May flowers

Lovely June

July Perfection

August Drinks

September Specials

October Events

November Vibes

December Days

Almost done with X Month ...

Happy XXX Month

Are you feelin the Spring vibes?

Happy Spring

Spring has sprung

Spring is officially here

Spring treat

Spring vibes

Are you feeling the Summer vibes?

Summer is officially here

Summer treat Summer vibes

Are you feeling the Fall Vibes?

Fall is officially here

Fall treat

Fall vibes

Are you feelin the Winter vibes?

Winter is officially here

Winter treat

Winter vibes

Winter warm up

7 YOUR PRODUCTS

Every coffee shop has their own style. Decide how you want your listings posted and go with that. You can always change your posting style depending on if it is working, new changes that evolve with posting options, or if you just want to change it up. You can vary the amount of detail in your posts including your shop address, phone number, emojis, or other information in posts about your store. In addition to the content you post, images are super important. This will catch the viewers eye as they scroll through social media.

BARRISTA

Meet our Barista

Barista recommendations

What is your Barista's favorite drink

What is your Barista making on certain days of the week

Barista facts and fun

What Is a Barista?

Interesting barista knowledge

Barista Magazine Online, content ideas here

World Barista Championship

Annual United States Barista Championship

Are your staff competing in any competitions upcoming? How did they do?

Find out who the Champions are!

BEANS

Describe the different coffee beans your shop sells

Terminology of different beans you sell

Purpose of the different beans you sell

What whole bean and ground products do you sell

If a customer buys a bag of your whole bean coffee, will you grind it for them

CAFFEINE

How much caffeine is in your different drinks

Which drinks come caffeine-free

How much caffeine is in a cup of coffee

Information about caffeine in various types of coffee

An easy solution to caffeine headache

Information about caffeine headaches

CAMPING

Camping with coffee

Essential coffee gear for camping, start with your shop's beans ☺

COFFEE DRINKS

Definitions of your products

Special flavors brought back throughout the year

The big reveal of a new product, post about this ahead of time

Describe your different coffees drinks

Non-Coffee drinks available for those who do not drink coffee

Iced coffee

Iced coffee cubes

Signature drinks or foods

Chilled or hot drinks – are there any that you sell so customers can try both and decide which they prefer

Caffeine free drinks

Gluten Free drinks

Keto drinks

Sugar free drinks

Vegan drinks

What is an Americano

Caffe Latte vs. Cafe Au Lait, do you know the difference

What Is a cappuccino

What's the difference between a cappuccino and a caffe latte

Why Is Columbian coffee so delicious

What is an espresso

How to drink espresso

What is a Latte

What is a macchiato

What is the difference between a cappuccino and espresso

What's in your frappes

What's in your smoothies

Have you ever wondered what the difference is between a coffeehouse vs a coffee shop

Ever wondered what exactly a coffee bar is

Descriptions

Acidity

African Coffee Beans

Arabica

Aroma

Bitterness

Body

Brazil Beans

Flavor

Robusta

Sumatra Beans

XXX is (describe the drink) with an image of the drink or if you want something sweeter order XXX which is (description of drink)

Describe your drinks with image of the drink and what is in it, for example Red Bull, syrups, fruit,

COFFEE FACTS

Interesting coffee facts

How is coffee processed

Growing altitude

Lower altitude beans

Producers, crops, regions in different countries

Coffee blends

USDA Organic

Where your coffee beans come from

Information about the farmers who farm the coffee

COFFEE GEAR AND ACCESSORIES

Your product line you carry for example coffee beans, travel mugs, mugs you sell

Your new products for example travel mugs, drinking mugs, plates and dishes, equipment

Your apparel

Equipment you sell for home brewing

Products that are sold out but on order

Tote bags with your logo on them. Post about your totes throughout the year to boost sales

Fun coffee accessories for everyone

Gift baskets

Hostess gifts

Last minute gift ideas

Ultimate Coffee Lovers Gift Basket

Your opinion of:
- Best coffee tools
- Coffee accessories not needed but great to have
- New products in the marketplace

CREAMER and MILK

Attributes of your creamers and milks

Describe the difference when you add milk to coffee

Describe your creamers

How your products are processed

Ingredients in your products for example frothed milk, cream, flavoring

New creamers you use

Organic

What do certain products taste like

What makes your creamers stand out

Where your creamer originates from

Why use almond milk

LATTE ART

Your coffee shops Latte Art

How you create it and images

Any information about the Latte Art at your shop

MENU

Your Menu

Breakfast items

Breakfast all day

Brunch items

Caffeine free drinks

Casseroles you serve

Changes to your menu

Chillin drinks

Coffee: Light roast, flavored coffee, organic coffee, decaf coffee choices

Decaf menu items

Dinner items on your menu

Featured flavors use an online digital tool to create image and describe flavor in your post

Fruit items on your menu

Gluten free products

Healthy drinks

Healthy foods

Hot chocolate

Ice cream, during the summer do you sell grocery store brands of ice cream single size cups

Ingredients available for sale

Ingredients in your products

Keto products you sell, food and drink

Last days to get limited time items on your menu

Light roast drinks

Limited time offerings of products on the menu, how long will they be available?

Low calorie drinks

Low calorie foods

Low carb drinks

Low carb food items

Lunch items

New blends you offer

New flavors

New items on your menu

New menu items and ingredients

New recipes

New releases

Organic products

Pairings of coffee and food

Pop Up Menu

Recommendations of what tastes great together

Sandwich of the day

Shirley Temple, if you serve them

Snacks on your menu

Soup of the day

Students love to study at coffee shops, post to encourage them to stop by

Sugar free drinks

The big reveal of a new product, give a heads up days before

Top selling drinks

Top selling food items, at different times of the day

Vegan menu items

Eye catching posts you can put together

What are the ingredients in the items on your menu, image of product

Which items are made from scratch

Seasonal menu

Seasonal Drinks

Spring Seasonal Menu

Summer Seasonal Menu

Winter drinks available in the summer

Fall Menu

Winter Menu

Your menu with prices so viewers know what the cost is if they visit your business

MUGS

Current coffee mugs and travel mugs

New mugs arriving soon

Best travel coffee mugs in your opinion

Custom Coffee Mugs You Design

Design Your Own Coffee Cup

Fun facts about coffee mugs

Great ideas for ways to reuse old coffee mugs

History of coffee mugs

How To Remove Stains From Coffee Mugs

Ways to recycle old coffee mugs

TEA DRINKS

Where your tea originates from

Tea flavors available

Hot Tea you sell

Iced Tea you sell

Organic tea

Tea that fits certain diets your customers follow

More Tea Posting Content

A treat for your sweet

Caffeine free drinks

Foods that pair perfectly with hot or cold tea

Fresh Batch of X tomorrow morning

Have you tried our … (insert what's inside)

New tea cups arriving soon

Signature tea drinks

Stop by to try our organic …

The big reveal of a new product, give a heads up days before

The perfect cup is waiting for you …

This month's specialty tea drink is …

TIPS

Did you know …

Home Brewing Tips, can be funny humor

How to brew at home

Information on how to make a great cup

Medical benefits linked to coffee

Tips on making product at home

What to do with leftover coffee

Why coffee groups are good for Seniors, social connections in retirement

WHAT IS SPECIAL ABOUT YOUR PRODUCTS

History of your ingredients

History of your products

Where do your products come from

Do any of your products have health benefits

Do you offer any products different from your competition

Post products online that can be ordered and either picked up or shipped

QUESTIONS FOR THE ENVIRONMENT

Are you using sustainable bags

Are you shipping in boxes that are reasonable

Do you compost

Do you have solar panels on your building

Do you recycle

Using less gas for deliveries

YOUR SHOP IS THE PERFECT PLACE TO

Celebrate

Get together with family

Have breakfast

Meet friends

Play a board game

Pickup drinks and food to go

Read a book

Read a magazine

Read the newspaper

Study

Work

Work meetings

Work on homework

8 COFFEE CONTENT

Sometimes you might be looking for some interesting information that brings customers and potential customers to your social media networks. If your goal is repeat visits, here are some ideas of other coffee related content to post about. Also, some the ideas below add to your expertise and can set you apart from your competition.

POST IDEAS

Anniversary Gifts

Birthday Gifts

Bring your book and relax with your favorite coffee

Click & Pickup available

Click & Ship available

Closed due to weather

Coffee humor

Coffee run for your office

Coffee slogans, fun parts of speech language, fun sayings

Come in and warm up...

Congratulations to the graduates of kindergarten, high school, community college, local college

Delivery of your products

Drink of the month

Drink that is on special during the month

Friendship Gifts

Grab it to go

Holiday products available to purchase

How do customers order ahead of time

Invitation posts, invite customers to stop by just because, for no specific reason

Keto Menu, how many choices do you have

Motivational quotes

New equipment

New month, new flavor of coffee

New month, new tea flavor

New month, stop by for a cup

Order ahead

Perfect for family functions

Perfect for office meetings

Pre-Order your items to go for day to day or holidays

Post reminders if you will not be offering a certain flavor any more, 1 week left, 2 days left

Products you sell, drinks, food and/or equipment

Return of favorite flavors

Saturday Mimosas and Bloody Mary's

Seasonal flavors available

SOLD OUT products

Start the month of ..... by trying ...

Stocking Stuffers

Sugar free drinks and food

Teacher Appreciation Gifts

Weather linked with your business

Website: link articles to your website

What you are roasting today

If your product is available in other cities, post about that city and location where it is sold

Why your product is special

Do you sell items like pies that people can buy and take to parties or serve at their own events

What you have in inventory remaining to sell and are now trying to move it

LOCAL BUSINESS KINDNESS

Gifts you gave to local businesses

Gifts you received from local businesses

Post about what is happening at a local business

Have a local business post about what is happening at your business

Links about what's happening in your town

Links for where to find the 'Best Of' for example the winners of the best restaurants in your area

9 CONVERSATIONS

Another way to encourage visitors to your social media networks is by asking questions. Keep in mind, if you ask a question, you might need to take the time to reply back in a timely manner. It is a great way to get your customers to engage and for folks from a distance away to get recommendations.

POST CONVERSATIONS THAT ENGAGE

Ask About Your Business

Best drink at your the coffee shop?

What is your favorite flavor of …?

Which artist/picture on display is your favorite?

What's happening tomorrow?

Which do you like better X bakery flavor or Y bakery products?

What is your favorite hot drink?

What is your favorite iced drink?

What drink goes best with X sandwich, X bakery item?

How do you take your coffee? Tea?

What makes the perfect espresso?

What is your favorite Spring Beverage? Summer, Fall, Winter

Vote for different items in your store that customers like, for example which picture, which new dishware, which table, which sitting area

Vote for your favorite cookie decoration

Vote for your favorite cupcake flavors

Have a map where customers can pin where they live in the US and are now visiting your coffeehouse

General Conversations

Are you ready for ...?   Snow, spring flowers, mowing the lawn

Best brunch restaurants?

Best business to visit?

Best Foodie Restaurant?

Best restaurant to watch sporting events at is ...

Does your family like to ...?

How do you dress up your ... food

How do you relax?

What is a great activity you participate in around here?

What is the most romantic restaurant in the area?

What is your favorite local restaurant?

What traditions do you have ...?

What's your favorite restaurant in this community?

Where can you go as a couple? As a family? With kids?

Would you prefer to eat x or y? For example stuffing or mashed potatoes at Thanksgiving

What are you thankful for?

What's your favorite brew at home? In the morning?

What do you drink during the day?

What good book are you currently reading?

What was your favorite childhood book?

What was your favorite snow day activity as a kid?

10 EVENTS

Posting events going on at your business and in the area is an excellent way to give great content and encourage repeat visits to your social media networks.

EVENTS

12 Days of Downtown

Advance Latte Art Class

Annual X Bazaar, spring bazaar, summer, fall, winter bazaar, small business bazaar, Health and Fitness bazaar

Annual golf outing

Banquet

Book Signings

Bring in businesses that have products that benefit your customers, ie Smart Home install, self-defense products, senior aging in place products

Buy a cup today and $# gets donated to X Charity

Can you guess what tomorrow is

Certain tv shows: favorite series, award shows, season finales, series finales

Christmas Party

Coffee and tea brew classes

Coffee Roasters Launch Party

Coffee and XXX Tasting at (time)! Stop by: do you have this on a regular schedule

Coffee tours

Comedy nights include the price of tickets and what is included in the price

Contest to name new ... flavor, bakery items,

Cookout

Cornhole Tournament

Customer Appreciation Event

Dance groups, artists painting in person, how to floral arrange, how to use technology

Discussion groups at your location for examples stock market discussion group

Double punch day, bring a friend

Drawings, giveaways, raffles

Elf on the shelf in your store to bring more customers in, come up with a year-round theme to draw in young kids with their parents

End of semester party

Facebook give away, post the winners

Favorite Mugs

Fill a Tray Day

First Wednesday of the Month sale on your product

XXX Flavor is back!

Friday Coffee Tasting: ... Free and open to all!

"Free and open to all" events

Fundraiser

Gingerbread House making

Giveaways

Giving Tuesday

Have classes after hours about how to make certain products, "Get your tickets here"

Holiday Bazaar

How to make Signature Drinks

Ice Cream Day – Sell delicious ice cream novelties Ice cream social

Instagram give away, post the winners

Join us for complimentary samples and treats

Kid book reading time

Kid friendly artists to perform around 9-10 am when small kids are available to get out

Last day for certain products you won't be carrying anymore

Last day of school

Latte Art Class

Launch events

Launch party

Live music

Local artists that sing, comedy, young students in band or orchestra, poetry, senior artistic groups

Local artists who bring their own keyboard for music or music and singing

Local artists on display at your business, some coffee shops rotate artists by month

Local community events

Local singers performing at your business

March Madness

Mark your calendar:

Missed our event, we have a repeat event at XXX, bring a friend

Monthly Brew Classes, signups and how much the fee is

Music type night on playlist: jazz, classic, instrumental, hiphop

New Equipment

New Menu Reveal

New week new school semester, local schools & colleges

Online auction

Open Mic

Outdoor furniture is back out, your patio is open, outdoor seating is open or soon to be open

Partner with other businesses who come to your area for their events

Pets up for adoption

Pool, run a fun one at your store, March Madness, season finale ending, local state sports competition, SuperBowl pool, make sure this is legal in your area

Private event availability

Raffle

Rescue Pets

Roasting Tour

Sales for Veterans, Veterans Day, Veterans get a discount on your food or coffee

Samplings

Save the date ...

School age kids reading time, SSR

Schools back in session, summer's over

Sip and Paint

Stop by when studying for finals for free cookies, totally free bring your friends

Stop in a Halloween costume and get a discount on your order

Stop in wearing red, white and blue and get a discount

Stop in with local team on your shirt and get a discount

Stop in if you are a Veteran or active duty military

Stop in if you are a first responder

SuperBowl Sunday

Taste of X, your business name, Taste of Spring, Summer, Fall, Winter, Taste of X (your City)

Teach customers how to make your products at home or how they are made

Teacher Appreciation items

Therapy pets, stop by to pet them

Tray day, fill a tray and get a discount

Treat yourself week

Trick or Treating for your customers at your business

Trivia Night

Ugly Sweater Day

Visiting Baristas or Chefs working at your location for the day or week

We are excited to roll out …

Weekday events

Weekend Events

What's happening in your community? Tie stopping in to your location to that event

Worship nights

YOU'RE INVITED! New flavor reveals, come in to taste and if you buy, you get free item with it

LOCATION

A place to get work done is at your business

Any satellite locations? Even for a weekend?

Are you going to be at another location on a specific day, popup location? Add hashtags if possible.

Articles in your newspaper that affect your area or your customers for example upcoming detours, new developments, growth, new school

Community events that help your customers for example senior workouts, free tutoring for students

Community events to go to then stop by for coffee Extended hours on certain days, maybe they are due to community events for example 4th of July Fireworks, local parade, holiday shopping

Gloomy outside today? Stop by for a cup

Invite customers to stop by after enrolling their kids in school, school events, sporting events, voting

Local awards given in your community, give a shout out to the winners

Other business' grand openings, post to help them out

Post about what other stores in your area are doing or have going on that week

Shopping at local stores? Stop by before or after at our coffee shop to relax

Speakers that are invited to your shop for events, hiking at local parks, hiking areas, bike trails, estate planning, history of the area

Spend your morning with us

Tie in stopping by your shop after visiting a community event

Tie in stopping by after schools out when there was a big event at the schools for example a play, special event during school, Pioneer Day, end of a weeklong project, fitness week

Tie in with professional sporting events

Tie in with local community events for example local sporting teams going to state, plays, dance recitals

What's happening in the community that you can partner with

Where will your food truck be located on certain days, post a schedule for customers to easily find you

PARTNERSHIPS

Partner with companies to boost each other's sales

Other businesses on your block

Other restaurants

Fresh flowers from a local business in images you post about your business, partnerships like that

Have a partnership with local businesses on certain times of the month, if you buy our product you receive a discount when you buy at a connected business

Highlight new businesses opening, ie grocery store, animal clinic, community buildings, parks

Welcome new businesses to your city

Other companies who bought and donated coffee gift cards for good causes such as Teacher Appreciation Day, Add the company's hashtag in your post

Holiday crafts you can make at your store for example something for Mother's Day or Father's Day for a cost $##/person

Who is coming to your town? Dance competitions, sports tournaments, association conferences, club meetings and more

Business of the Month: vote on social media for a business who would get free coffee brought to them.

SALES

Are you in a coupon book or app? Post to let people know to look for your coupon and save

Buy a gift certificate and get a free cup coupon

Cheers to a long weekend, % discount

Coupons

Customer Appreciation Day

Drawing for people who drop their business card in a drawing box

eGift cards, maybe certain days discount the card

Early Bird Sales

Encourage kid's reading, school age kids reading time, SSR, discount on purchase

Free cup of coffee with a donation to a cause that you are promoting

Frequent customer punch cards, double punch days

Free cups of coffee for groups ie veterans, teachers, first responders on certain days of the year

Fundraisers at your location

Gift cards

Gift certificates

Giveaways

Holiday sales

Holiday gift cards, eGift cards for Valentines Day, Mothers Day, Fathers Day, 4th of July etc.

Mention this post and receive X% off any xxx

New month new specials

Pair with local businesses, your coffee or tea packages at their business and their products for example plants at yours, candy shop, art work

Restaurant Week

Senior discount

Spring Break sale for those who did not go anywhere

Stop by wearing X and receive $# off your order for example ugly sweater, super hero shirt, sports team shirt, red white and blue clothing

Student discount

Valentine's Day Sale

Voting discount

Winners of drawings for free product

Spring Sale

Summer Sale

Fall Sale

Winter Sale

Buy a bag of coffee and get a free cup

Buy a gift card for $50 and get a free cup

Buy a mug to benefit your local zoo (or other business) and get a free cup of coffee

Buy a 'fundraiser for a good cause' mug and get a free cup of coffee

BOGO

Giveaways linked with charities you support in your community for example schools, zoos, parks

Raffles

Tray day, discounts for tray orders

Do you offer a discount if customers bring in their own cup? If customers bring in their own cup, do you take a photo and post if it is a cute cup

Mention this post and get #% off your purchase, limit one per customer

Discount for two drinks purchased, encourages meetings at your shop

Give a heads up post about upcoming sales the next week

Multiple punch days to generate sales of slow moving drinks for example double punch day or triple punches

Discount when you reach # followers on each of your social media networks

Percent of sales on a certain day donated to certain causes

11 IMAGES

Images Make All The Difference! Also the quality of the Images is very important.

Keep in mind not everyone likes coffee so make sure you include images of non-coffee products to bring in customers.

Use online graphics design tools to add eye catching information to your images or to create images. Canva is a great tool but there may be another one you prefer

Add emoji's to your images
Link your images to your website or blog

IMAGES ABOUT YOUR BUSINESS

Menu images

Coffee images

Tea images

Food images

Your staff/team

Your product

Different flavors of your products

Your staff creating the product

Your staff holding a completed product

Your staff selling

Your staff serving

Your staff meetings

New hires, stop by to greet

Inside of your business

Outside of your building

Gift certificates

eGift Cards

Coupons

Pop up locations by your business

Who works each day: Monday Crew, Tuesday Crew, Wednesday Crew, Weekend Crew

Barista's Latte Art

When you are at conferences, association meetings, or receiving certifications

You and your customers at your business

Your customer's pets

Your products

Your brand name products

Your products ingredients

Your products ingredients with the drink and the branded product next to it

Your prices

A product with the price listed

Images of where your product comes from

Image of possible new products you may carry to see if your customers would buy them

Seasonal drinks

For weekends, take a photo of a great cup of coffee with your shop in the background showing a spot where your customers can sit and relax either alone or catching up with a friend

Animals that are around your business for example a bird that hangs around often

Baked items

Bakery display with all of your product in it

Bazaar Happenings

Changes to your shop from start to finish, anything from new dishes to outdoor seating

Close up of empty seating areas customers can choose as a destination spot at your business

Close up of your clean and empty coffee cups

Close up of your cooler for what you offer ie drinks, parfaits, yogurt, fruit, desserts

Coffee of the Month

"Coffeeology"

Coffee On The Go

Coffee To Go Box

Community events

Customers involved in your coffee and tea brewing classes or tasting events

Customer's bikes, "Bike to your shop for a cup!"

Customer's office with your travel cup at their desk

Customers who purchase gifts for others

Decaf drinks

Delivery vehicle

Drive through window, if you have one

Early morning food specials

Funny coffee memes

Gift baskets you sell

Gifts you receive from customers

Gifts you receive from other businesses

Giveaways

Gluten free drinks

Holiday drinks such as colors, flavors, decorations

Holiday foods you carry, holiday decorated foods

How your business celebrates holidays

How your business receives advance orders

How your product looks when it is purchased for example your shopping bag with product in it

Images of young customers who come by with their parents

Images of what your location used to be used for

Images of your coffee cup with logo at different places around your city

Games you have in your shop available to use when you stop

Kids menu

Landscaping around your business with your logo on a cup/mug in the photo

Line of cars in your drive through in the morning

Line of cars in your drive through in the afternoon

Live events you host

Local artists work on display at your shop

Low carb menu items

Men's groups that stop by on a regular basis

Menu board

Menu changes

Menu items

Movie Characters with your coffee cup in the picture for example Frozen, Star Wars

New equipment

New plates, mugs, cups your business will use

Non-Coffee items

Notes your customers leave you

Online store products

Orders ready to go, coffee

Orders ready to go, food

Organic drinks

Outdoor seating

Outdoor views around your business

Outside seating with your drink on the table

Pair a drink with a food item

People wearing your coffee shop logo apparel

Pet images with your customers who stop by

Picture of empty meeting room, study spaces, game room,

Picture of full room filled with customers meeting, studying, open mic

Picture of your business at sunrise with the lights on

Plaid Day

Product line you sell, bagged, bottles, totes, apparel

Rainbow in the sky above or by your shop

Salute to care givers

Salute to First Responders

Salute to Military

Salute to stay at home parents

Senior Groups who stop by on a regular basis

Sky above your shop

Snow around your shop

Social media networks

Spell words with coffee beans on your tables for example "We Love You"

Staff dress up days, Valentine's Day, 4th of July

Sugar free drinks

Ultimate Coffee Lovers Gift Pack

Unique parts of your business for example do your windows open? Can your seating change?

Vegan items

Vegetarian items

VIP Card

Wildlife outside your shop

Workstations available at your location, images with customers working and empty spots

Your apparel

Your customers who meet for regular reasons, after an event ie farmers market, pickleball, school event

Your coffee cup held by a hand outside of your business

Your eGift Card

Your gift card

Your staff roasting coffee

Your travel cups getting prepared, so visitors know they can get it to go

Seasonal Images

Spring Favorites + menu image

Summer Favorites + menu image

Fall favorites + menu image

Winter favorites + menu image

Holiday decorations at your location

Spring Specials

Summer Specials

Fall Specials

Winter Specials

Drink with holiday decorations

Drink with seasonal food items you sell

Images That Highlight Your Area

Historic old photos of the area

Local artists work

Local beautiful areas

Local community assets

Local historic areas

Local parks

Local sunrises

Local sunsets

Other points of interest within a designated perimeter

VIDEOS

A day at your shop, speed up the video to show Coffee beans getting roasted

Drive through traffic

How busy you are

Live bands

Local events such as parades

Open Mic events

Pets that stop by

Staff getting ready for the day

Staff dancing or singing

Staff question and answer video, get to know them

Your menu items from the beginning to the end when it is ready to sell/eat

ONLINE GRAPHICS ART TOOL

Create fun images you can use that are not photos

Closed, change in business hours

Good Morning with a coffee cup and sunshine

Holidays

Humor

information on top of the image

Motivational sayings

New hours or other changes in business hours

Promotions

Quotes

Sales

Take a photo of a menu item and add the name of the item on the image so when you post is being viewed and read. The reader reads the description and sees what it looks like. Add emoji's for more description and fun to the image.

Use an online graphics art tool to add eye catching slogans, shop logo, name of the drink, name of the food, flowers, sun, seasonal symbols on your image for more impact

12 YOUR BUSINESS

Your Business

Post about your business

Post your Mission Statement

Hours of operation, address, phone number, website link

Add your phone number so potential customers can contact you

Add your website URL in your posts

We appreciate your business post

Have more questions about …? Call us at 555-555-1212 or visit our website!

Do you sell K-cups, bags of beans, tea, and more

Your company logo on the corner of the image

Gift Cards

eGift Cards

Gift certificates

Post a day before or more in advance when you will be closed so people can change plans if they were going to your business when you will be closed

Frequent customer punch card

Post about "Double Punch Days" 2 punches for 1 purchase

Post about double order days, 4 punches for 2 purchases

Do you have a Pay-It Forward board? Customers can pay for a cup of coffee for military or first responders. When that military or first responder comes in for a cup of coffee and shows their ID, it has already been paid for.

What is special about your business?

Historic location

History of your business

Unique furniture

Plants and landscaping

Delivery, do you offer free delivery with # cups purchased or a certain dollar amount

Drive through window

Pull up parking spot for quick pickup

Items on your menu that fit your customer's foods, drinks, special diets, and ingredients requirements.

Anything happening in the community where you can set up a popup location? Dance competitions, competitions at local schools or universities, at other businesses

Are you open during holidays?

Are you open if there is bad weather predicted?

Are you setting up temporary spot with your product for local events, ie 5K run coffee for the audience, where is your location and hours you will be open

Changes within your business, new plants, new furniture, new art, new mugs

Classes you provide

Coffee of the Month

Coffee to go box

Delivery information, hours, quantity for free delivery, do you deliver drinks and food?

Company's anniversary, Anniversary Week

Company's birthday, Birthday Week

Barista favorites

Birthday Drawing and Giveaway

Staff birthdays or anniversaries

Staff favorites

Staff parties or employees dressing up in holiday apparel for example ugly sweater or Halloween costumes

Tastings at certain times of the week or month

Changes to your business such as remodeling post your progress

Destination Party location, do you have separate room availability

Fundraising or collecting for area relief efforts

Fundraiser results, thank you opportunity

Holiday Hours, changes in business hours

How many types of products to you offer, for example 'Over 15 Gluten Free Drink Choices'

How your products are made

International Coffee of the Month

New locations

Non-coffee drinker items for those who like to get together with coffee drinkers

Rewards card

Unusual times you will be closed for example for staff training

VIP card

Do you offer food or drink ready to grab and go then head to community events: outside music, kids sporting events, high school events, biking, community events for example bento boxes, food for away youth sports games, make it easy for parents and customers to grab and go

Post about if you have meeting rooms, an upstairs, different areas in your business that could be used for certain purposes: studying, business meetings, hobby groups, kid-friendly area, game area for cards or board games

Post if you have an order ready to go

Post about orders for customer's office, meetings, residential, drinks and food boxed up

Post about your delivery vehicle

What is your advance order notice in order to deliver, 24 hours?

Do you deliver food before/during local events such as basketball games, dance competitions, outdoor sports events, tournaments, worksites, all-day events, and at other locations?

Is there road construction where customers may not be able to get to your location. Give the detour directions or a map about how to reach your shop

Your Quality of Work

Additional training classes attended

Awards you, your staff, or your company received including the photo of you holding your award

Coffee education you have

Conferences you attended for example Coffee Fest, National Coffee Association

Nominations your business or staff received

Number of years have you been in business

Product awards received

Testimonials, post with permission

Trips your business takes

Voted Best of XXX, post more than once if you receive these accolades

Nominations

when your business is nominated for an award, ask for votes. Include the way your customers can vote for example Vote Here: URL

About You

Keep in mind how visitors will view what you post. The goal is to grow your business, not reduce it.

About Me Post, link it back to your blog

Any personal awards, not business related

Charities you support

Post any high review ratings you receive

Volunteering you do

Who You Work With

Additions to your Team

Welcome post of new staff who joined the organization

Is your business hiring staff or team members

Your staff's volunteering programs, things they are involved in

Are you at any Farmers Markets or in other stores you can post about?

Do you partner with a local bakery who delivers fresh bakery items to your shop? Post about what they brought today to create a following as people are curious what is available today and watch for when certain bakery items return to your store for sale

YOUR PRODUCTS

Have any of your products received an award

Anything you sell show up in a magazine or on tv?

Do you sell items that save your customers time from shopping for gifts or club/charity gifts items, ie Lions Club bags of Nuts, Local Artwork hanging on your walls, seasonal items, gluten free coffee

What do you offer to the Senior customers?

Do you deliver your coffee and bakery to their location?

13 MORE CONTENT IDEAS

OTHER IDEAS FOR CONTENT TO POST

The idea with this chapter is for you to find happenings of interest to your customers. By you completing the "legwork", your customers will check your social media often to find out "what's happening". In turn, hopefully organic shares will cause additional followers to your social media networks.

Your Community

Annual charity events in your community

Best things to do in (your city) this weekend

Create your own video to highlight what's great about the community

Free admission to events in your area at certain times throughout the year

Fun runs in your community

fun things to do in ... (your town)

News articles: upcoming detours, school achievements, student athletes heading to state competitions

Openings of new businesses, grocery stores, post office, malls, schools, restaurants

Organizations in your area that are fundraising, sponsoring charities, ie school supplies for kids

Parade videos (Homecoming parades, 4th of July parades)

Phone videos of things happening in your area for example tree lighting, 5K run winners, sporting events

Special deals in your community

What's going on at other local businesses for example Lions Club Nuts Sale stand

Accolades of company

Charity Awareness Month

Chili Cook-off for charity

Ease into spring

Ease into summer

Ease into fall

Ease into winter

Foundations you support

Holiday recipes

Images to go with national days

Images of beautiful places around your town

Pet images

Post about you and your family if you want

Recipes

Seasonal changes – Fall is here, Spring is here,

Short videos of other content you find interesting,

Tailgate for a Cause

Websites with great content ideas, work related, and fun ideas

Welcoming sports figures who join local teams for example NFL new players

What's happening this weekend

When to plant spring flowers

14 HASHTAGS

#Hashtags

Hashtags can help your posts get found at a subject related central spot. If someone is looking for a coffee shop in the area, they may be following a particular hashtag on a social media network and then they may discover you. The goal with social media hashtags is that potential customers will begin following your specific social media posts because they like your content. People who are following that hashtag on the social media channel will see your post or share it with a friend.

However, always check the hashtag before using it. Sometimes a particular hashtag may not be currently used or it may have content that does not reflect your business goals.

PERSONALIZED HASHTAGS

@your business hashtag
#your business hashtag

#(your company name)

#(your city name)

#(your state name)

#(your neighborhood)

#(your business name)

#(your business name)brew

#(your business name)cafe

#(your business name)coffee

#(your business name)

#(your business name)gatheringspace

#(your business name)breakfast

#(your business name)brunch

#(your city name)

#(your city name)brew

#(your city name)cafe

#(your city)coffee

#(your city)coffeeshop

#(your city)favorites

#(your state)coffee

#(your state)locallyownedcoffeeshop

#coffeeshop(your city)

#onlyin(your city)

#thisis(your city)

#(state)proud

#(your county)county

COFFEE RELATED HASHTAGS

#almondmilk

#americano

#anniversary

#artofmakingcoffee

#barista

#baristalove

#bestcoffee

#bestdonuts

#birthday

#blendeddrinks

#blendedlattes

#breakfast

#breakfastcasserole

#brew

#brunch

#butfirstcoffee

#buylocal

#cafe

#caffeine

#cappuccino

#caramel

#coconutmilk

#coffeeaddict

#coffeeallday

#coffeeandmusic

#coffeebar

#coffeebreak

#coffeefamily

#coffeeforlife

#coffeeholic

#coffeeislove

#coffeelover

#coffeelovers

#coffeemaker

#coffeeroaster

#coffeerun

#coffeeshop

#coffeetime

#coldbrew

#coldbrewcoffee

#craftcoffee

#dairyfree

#discount

#dontforgetthecoffee

#drinklocalcoffee

#eathealthy

#espresso

#falldrinks

#familytime

#farmtocup

#funweekend

#freshcoffee

#frap

#frappe

#frappicino

#getcaffeinated

#GivingTuesday

#glutenfree

#homemadegoodies

#hotchocolate

#hotcoffee

#icedcoffee

#IcedCoffeeEveryday

#icedlattes

#justcoffee

#Keto

#ketobreakfast

#ketocoffee

#ketodiet

#ketofriendly

#ketotransformation

#Latte

#LatteArt

#latteartdaily

#limitedtime

#localshop

#lovefrapps

#macchiato

#mondaymorninglocalbrew

#muffins

#onsale

#organic

#organiccoffee

#pastries

#peppermint

#pumpkin

#raffle

#recharge

#roasterinresidence

#sale

#seasonaldrinks

#shoplocal

#smallbusiness

#soymilk

#specialtycoffee

#specialtydrinks

#springdrinks

#stressrelief

#sugarfreedrinks

#summerdrinks

#supportlocal

#supportsmallbusiness

#tea

#theartofmakingcoffee

#thankyou

#timeforcoffee

#treatyourself

#vegan

#winterdrinks

HOLIDAYS

#endofquarter

#NewYear

#MartinLutherKingJrDay

#MLK

#MLKDay

#ValentinesDay

#PresidentsDay

#StPatsDay

#StPatricksDay

#AprilFoolsDay

#MemorialDay

#MothersDay

#Graduation

#FathersDay

#IndependenceDay

#4thofJuly

#LaborDay

#NewSchoolYear

#NationalCoffeeDay

#Halloween

#VeteransDay

#Thanksgiving

#hanukkah

#christmaseve

#Christmas

#newyearseve

#HappyHolidays

FOOD RELATED

#(city)foodies

#(city)eats

#yelp(city)

#breakfast

#brunch

#lunch

#dinner

#delicious

#eatlocal

#foodblog

#foodie

#foodlover

#foodlovesme

#foodphotography

#foodporn

#healthy

#healthyfood

#organic

#sandwich

#soup

#tastyeats

#veggie

#veggies

#veggiesandwich

#yum

#yummy

DAYS OF THE WEEK HASHTAGS

#Monday (s)

#HappyMonday

#MondayMorning

#MondayMotivation

#Tuesday (s)

#Wednesday (s)

#Thursday (s)

#ThrowbackThursday

#Friday (s)

#Saturday (s)

#saturdayvibes

#Sunday (s)

#SundayThoughts

#Weekend

#GoodMorning

SPORTS TEAMS

#(local school teams)

#SuperBowl

#MarchMadness

#Masters

#StanleyCup

#WorldSeries

#FIFA

#(NFL team)

#(NBA team)

#(NHL hockey team)

#(soccer team)

#(MLB team)

#(local college & university teams)

15 RESOURCE WEBSITES

WEBSITES WITH GREAT CONTENT FOR YOUR POSTS

- Coffee-brewing-methods.com
- Coffeechronicler.com
- Coffeegeek.com
- Coffeeowlsociety.com
- CoffeeTalk.com
- Creatorsofcoffee.com
- FreshCup.com
- Perfectdailygrind.com
- Sprudge.com

- https://emojipedia.org/
- https://getemoji.com/

YouTube Videos

Latte Art

Baristas

Other coffee shops making a difference around the country or world

About the Author

Danielle McCorkle has worked in social media for a number of years. She has posted on many social media networks for different companies. As a manager of eCommerce, her experience includes managing and sometimes setting up ecommerce sites Amazon.com, Walmart.com, Jet.com, eBay.com and other eCommerce sites. In addition, the author has used search term programs, managed marketing campaigns, and worked with other social media companies. She received a Bachelor's of Science in Retail from the University of Wisconsin-Madison.